WRITERS REPUBLIC

A TRUE STORY OF A
DOMESTIC
VIOLENCE
SURVIVOR

How a woman survived domestic and physical abuse

COURTENY MUDGE

WRITERS REPUBLIC L.L.C.
515 Summit Ave. Unit R1
Union City, NJ 07087, USA

Website: *www.writersrepublic.com*
Hotline: *1-877-656-6838*
Email: *info@writersrepublic.com*

Ordering Information:
Quantity sales. Special discounts are available on quantity purchases by corporations, associations, and others. For details, contact the publisher at the address above.

Library of Congress Control Number: 2021909025
ISBN-13:   978-1-63728-410-0   [Paperback Edition]
                      978-1-63728-411-7   [Digital Edition]

Rev. date: 04/29/2021

DEDICATION

To my husband Tim Mudge, who supported me and helped me in more ways than one. I was beyond broken when we got together, but he put me back together. He is an amazing man I am so blessed.

To my children, who all in their own way help me continue to smile and remind me every day that I can't give up. I would've been so lost without them; they are my world.

To my mother, who always believed in me and loved me no matter what. I wasn't the perfect daughter, but she was an amazing mother. I miss her so much.

To my sister, who has been there for me. She always accepted me no matter how many times I messed up.

To my past. I have had a horrible past, but it taught me so much. And now, because of my past, I have the opportunity to help others, save others, and more.

I also owe a sense of gratitude to everyone at Writers Republic who has worked with me and published my book.

INTRODUCTION

My name is Courteny and this is the true story of my life. I want to share my life story because I don't want anyone to go through what I have gone through. And for those who are still and are in this situation, I hope my story will help save them and give them the courage to leave.

No one deserves to be hit. No one deserves to be abused. I thought Luke was one of kind—he swept me off my feet and caught me when I wasn't expecting it. Every time he gets me, it was always a good one. But he wasn't charming or anything like that. When he got into drugs and drinking, he would beat me a good one and put me through hell and then some.

I will get to all that. But I will start from the beginning. You will now read about my true life story, my experiences, how I survived, and more. So, get comfortable.

CHAPTER
ONE

I was born on January 19, 1989. My mother's name was Diane and she was a single mother. My father left when I was three weeks old. I never met him, and he never came back nor did I ever hear from him again.

My mother did an amazing job, and I have nothing bad to say about her. I was her only child until I turned six years old, when she had my little sister. It was always just the three of us. Of course, my mom had boyfriends, but they never stayed around for long. Now, as you can imagine, being a single mother raising two girls was hard for my mother, but she never complained. She always made sure that we were happy, fed, had a place to live, and more.

We did move around a lot. Although it was hard, it was not too bad. *Yes*, life was great. Until I turned twelve and my life changed, and so did I. I went backwards for years and struggled while my family abandoned me permanently.

I am a woman who survived abuse and abandonment. A woman who struggled with mental disorders, and has been in mental institutions asking for help. Yet, I still came out as a great person, a great woman that still smiles every day. I am in my second marriage, I have children, and I could not be happier. I have succeeded in life and I am so proud of myself. I'm telling my story to help and encourage others, to let others know they are not alone, to stay positive, and to not give up no matter what.

One thing I learned in life is that it is too short. And that no matter what happened or what you have been through, you can still accomplish anything in life. As long as you set your mind to it. Trust me, you can still be a great person, you can still be happy, and more. You are strong enough to get through everything you will go through.

For a long time, I thought I deserved being abused and that I was weak and useless. It took me years to realize that I did not deserve any of that—that I am strong enough to stand back up and move forward.

CHAPTER
TWO

We were living in Sherburne, New York, when I turned twelve years old. We were living next door to my uncle's fiancée. We were living in the country and had a lot of cookouts. We were enjoying the country life, and we were all happy. But then one night, it all changed. One night, my mom ordered pizza.

Since my mother does not drive, my uncle's fiancée took my mom and sister to go get the pizza while I stayed at home. Shortly after they left, my uncle showed up and asked me where everyone was. I told him where they went. He then sat down and started talking to me. He was drunk and was still drinking. He asked if he could get a hug and I gave him one. But then he kissed me. I tried to get away, but he would not let go. He started French kissing me. Good thing I was able to stop him and got away.

Then a few minutes later, my mom was back. *Thank God*! I asked her if we could talk in private and so we did. I told her what my uncle did to me. She called my school the next day and asked for help to report it. My school counselor spoke with me. They called the cops and CPS. I told them what happened and my uncle also admitted what he did. However, once my family found out, shit hit the fan.

They took my uncle's side and told me I was a liar, a whore, and that I only said it to get attention. *It hurt me so much.* Then my family abandoned me, started holding grudges, and started to not have anything to do with me. I will never understand why they took his side even though he admitted it all. My mom told them that she believed me. We had to move again.

We moved a lot. Growing up, I had been to fifteen different schools, so I had friends all over. We may have moved around a lot, but my mom was always great in keeping me and my sister happy. We got to see a lot of towns and meet new people, and see different things. So moving around a lot had its plus sides as well as its downsides. I have always told myself that if all else fails, I would have a successful career as a mover. I told my mom about it and all she did was laugh at me.

CHAPTER
THREE

Now, as you can imagine, I was a mess after what my uncle did, and on top of that, I was a mess after what my family said. The only one who stayed around and believed in me, besides my mom, was my grandmother. A few years passed by and I was in counseling. I got touched five more times and was also raped. Now these had happened with men my mom knew.

She thought they were all her friends. Although they all had a history of touching and raping children, my mom, being the kind-hearted woman, believed they had all changed and wouldn't do it again. She left me alone with those men and they touched me. One of them also raped me. For years, I was angry at my mother. For years, I had blamed her and more. It took me years to make my peace with that.

By the time I did, it was too late. You will understand why I say this later. Again, my family ran their mouths about me. They hated me even more. I became suicidal and was in a mental institution two different times for help. I was a wreck for many years. I admit I put my mom through hell. I was not the perfect daughter, but I did not ask for all that to happen to me.

It ruined me, made me a wreck, and more. My family did not see it that way. For years I did all that I could to get them back in my life. I tried changing myself, but nothing worked. They kept holding grudges, kept putting me down, etc. My mom kept telling me to forget about them and that we didn't need them because that is not what family does to other family members. That I was better off without them and so on.

She would tell me this for years. But it took me years to understand it, to realize that she was right. What my family did to me did not help me for years. While I was growing up, it was not easy for me. It was really hard. And again, I put my mom through hell—I admit that.

I had gone through so much that made me a wreck. I never asked for all that to happen to me, but my family saw it as me looking for attention and me as a liar. It would have been nice if they had supported me better. But, of course, they did not. That would have been too much to ask. With my family, you had to be perfect and you had to make great money.

If you were anything less than that, then you didn't matter. It was a really harsh expectation to live up to because of my issues and so on. As far as my family was and is concerned, I was dead to them. I was not even a part of the family—in their eyes.

CHAPTER

FOUR

When I was sixteen years old, my mom finally moved us back to my hometown and it made me so happy. My home is in DeRuyter, New York. I started dating and, because I was in special ed, I went to another school. If you have ever been to DeRuyter, you know how small the town is. This was when I met a guy who was very sweet and all the girls wanted him.

He was way out of my league, but he would always talk to me. We would give each other a hug. He would dance with me at school dances. He taught me how to do the watermelon crawl. He made my days at school so much better, but as always after you graduate school, you lose contact with a lot of people.

The guys I went out with were complete jerks. A few years went by; I turned 18 years old and moved into my own apartment. I was behind on my rent and the landlord evicted me. I was trying to find a place to live. I was not able to move back in with my mom because her place was way too small. On New Year's Eve, a friend of mine set me up on a blind date with a man named Luke. This is where my story and life got more interesting and harder.

He offered me to move in with him. Me, being desperate and having nowhere else to go, accepted his offer. Luke was 20 years older than me at the time. I saw him only as a friend. But after moving in with him, after becoming friends and getting closer to him, that all changed and we started dating.

While we were dating, he treated me great, although we had fights. Shortly after we started dating, I found out my mom had cancer. After two years of dating, Luke and I got married on March 2010. That's when everything changed.

Luke had an ex-wife and four kids with her. So, I had my hands full. His ex-wife and four kids always caused drama. They would run their mouths and were beyond noisy. Shortly after we got married, Luke started drinking again. I was going back and forth to my aunt's house to babysit while she helped my mom.

I was at my mom's house here and there, but because of my aunt, I could not be there for my mom like I wanted to be. When she found out she had cancer, it was already stage four. The doctors only gave her two weeks to live but she was able to fight it for two more years. She had seven different types of cancer.

She was in her late 30s when she was diagnosed, and she lost her battle to cancer in January 2011 in her early 40s. I was seven months pregnant with my first child at the time. She had never got the chance to meet her grandson. I remember when it was time to say goodbye to her and I told her I was so sorry for how I was growing up. I told her I was sorry for hurting her, for not being a perfect daughter. I said was sorry for being angry with her for so many years.

She said she forgave me and that she loves me. And that she was sorry, too. I also helped her put her hands on my stomach; she was so weak. She talked to her grandson and said goodbye to him. She said sorry to him for not being able to hold on until he was born. She told him she loved him, and that she was so excited to be a grandmother.

She made me promise that all my kids knew about her. I have kept that promise and always will. I went to her calling hours and wanted to be at the funeral but my aunt wanted me to go home knowing I had no ride back from her funeral the next day. And so I missed it, and until this day it hurts me. Of course, my aunt, the jerk she is, told my family that I did not want to be there. And my family believed it.

My sister then went to live with our other aunt. I did not get a lot of my mom's stuff after she died, thanks to my family. No, I do not blame my sister for it. After this, my sister and I started to lose touch because of my family. Our family brainwashed her, messed her up bad. But she gets out of there. Thank God! And she never looked back.

CHAPTER
FIVE

Two months after my mom died, I had my baby boy. I was still married to Luke, and my mom absolutely hated him. I didn't understand why until years and years later. Like I said, Luke started drinking shortly before we got married and continued. He was in and out of prison. We were always living with his parents expect for the few times we actually had our own place.

Three years later, we had another baby together. Of course, his ex-wife and his other kids said my boys were not Luke's. His ex-wife had no rights to talk because none of her kids with Luke are his, and my boys were proven to be Luke's.

I always believed in my heart that he would stop drinking. That I could get him to stop. I always believed that if I did all that I can to make him happy, he would stop. But he never did. His ex-wife and other four kids were always starting trouble as they always do. They always run their mouths and more daily. So, there was always drama and stress.

I dealt with this for nine years. And because of his drinking, he got abusive and he had good control over me. He brainwashed me, and me a horrible person. I dealt with it for years. He would slam me on the floor, throw me across the room, hit me, and more.

There was this one time when I woke up and there was a giant snake on me. I am terrified of snakes Luke knew about this. So, that morning he was holding down a giant snake on me. I didn't remember much after waking up and seeing the snake's eyes were looking at me. A day later,

I woke up and I was in the hospital. I had passed out from the shock. Luke claims it was a joke. Yeah, well his joke put me in shock and in the hospital. *Some joke.* He never once said sorry.

It had gotten worse when he was using drugs. We were married for seven years and have been together for nine years before I got the courage and the strength to leave him. I didn't care what he did to me, but when he got violent with our boys, that was where I said, "Enough is enough." And left him. I had to call the cops in order to leave him because he said I was not taking our boys. It took three state troopers and one cop to be able to get me and my boys out of there. But we got out of there.

I stayed with a friend until they kicked me out. After that, I got my own place. I was on public assistance due to the domestic violence and I couldn't work. Plus, my boys were struggling. So, I stayed home to help them heal and I was getting help to heal myself as well.

CHAPTER
SIX

This was my new life with my boys after leaving Luke. Now, after being in a domestic violence situation for so long, it took me a long to time to adjust to my new life without it. But once I did, *Oh my god*, I could not believe the difference. Luke did everything he could to get me to come back, but I never did and filed for divorce. A domestic violence survivor never forgets what they been through. It changes them, makes them more guarded, it haunts them for a long time, and so on.

Until this day, what I went through still gets to me. And when I feel the right side of my face, I would see how bad my right eye is and how it will never be the same. I always remember how it happened. I remember him having me kidnapped just to prove his point. How he use to fix my vehicles to have serious issues that was supposed to kill me. When I feel the top of my hands, I feel how they are and how they will never be the same again.

I remember it all; everything that he did to me. It does not and will never go away. I still have nightmares about the years I was with him, but I do the best I can to not have it affect my happiness now. That's why I share my story and experience from domestic violence. To help others, to save others, to give them courage and hope, to let them know they're not alone and never will be, that you can do it. And to not stay in a bad situation.

At this time, we have joint custody of our boys. I had the residential custody. Luke sees our boys on weekends. However, on one weekend,

11

a really horrible thing happened to our youngest boy. Luke was drunk and had a bonfire, he had pushed our son into the bonfire.

The next day, he messaged me saying that our son had burned himself. I asked how bad, and he said it was not that bad. It had taken me three hours to get Luke to send me a picture of the burn, and when he did, I flipped out. I asked Luke if he took him to the ER and he had said 'No'.

I asked how it happened, he told me and I flipped. I rushed to his place to get my boys. After I left, I took our youngest to the ER. He had second degree burns on his hand. The doctor in the E.R had called C.P.S. And nothing was found on me or against me. I was cleared.

After this, I took Luke back to court to make a court order that he was no longer allowed to drink while the boys visited him. After this, he didn't see them very much. Then one weekend, four months after my youngest boy's burn injury, Luke took our boys again, and this time our youngest boy had broken his wrist in his father's care. So, CPS got involved again.

This time, he didn't see much of our boys because his beer and drugs were much more important than our boys. Now, all I ever wanted was for him to be a father. I just wanted my boys to have their father. But that was asking too much. People say I'm at fault, too while some people say it's not my fault at all. Everyone has their own opinion about it.

In April, I ran into a guy I used to go to school with. To my surprise, it was the same guy that I used to hug in school. The one that always danced with me at school dances. The same one that taught me the watermelon crawl. I was so shocked to see him again after all this time. Immediately, we started talking and catching up.

And later on, I came to find out that he always had a crush on me like I did with him. He said I was the one that got away. We started dating shortly after that, and my boys adored him. We then found out I was three weeks pregnant a little over a month later. Shortly after finding out I was pregnant, he moved in with me.

CHAPTER
SEVEN

When my mom died, I didn't break down. I couldn't break down because in Luke's eyes, that was weakness. For years, I could not look at her pictures. I could not even talk about her. Four years after her death, I had a major meltdown. I was angry with myself for being angry with her for years, for not forgiving her sooner. I had lost so many years with her because of how angry I was with her.

When I was having my melt down, I felt like I was crazy because I could see her. I had beyond-horrible nightmares and I could not look at myself. I couldn't even smile. I thought I had all the time in the world to make it all up to her, but, nope, I was wrong. When I finally forgave her and made peace with it all, she died and was gone forever. She was and is an amazing woman. A beyond-amazing mother.

She is my inspiration. She was always smiling. She had a heart of gold. I would give anything to have had more time with her. This is what I struggle with since she died. I just cannot seem to forgive myself for it. Yes, she forgave me before she died but that's not the point. I miss her so much.

Everyone keeps telling me that I will be okay but I'm not going to ever get over her. And I probably never will forgive myself; but I will keep trying to because I know that's what she would want. Word of advice don't ever stay angry at anyone for long because you will never know how much time you have left with them. Now, after my mom died, I did manage to learn to stick up for myself, speak my mind, and more.

Here's a poem that I have written for my mom. If you have lost a loved one, you can relate to it.

I Miss You

I had just heard the horrible news and fell to the floor
So I called you today just to hear your answering machine
Say you are not around
Oh, you are not around
You can call me crazy but I just had to hear your voice again
With the memories of you
And the sun in the sky I am all alone again
I wanna tell you the weather is fine
I wanna tell you I can't get you off my mind
And I wish you were here with me
Don't you know
I really miss you
Yes, I do,
Yeah
I miss you

Shortly after my mom died, I was finally able to tell two of my aunts and that felt great. I was also able to accept not having a family.

I finally said,

"Screw them, their lost not mine."

Because despite my past, I am a great person. I am worthy enough and I don't need to kiss their butts to have them in my life. I don't always have to change my self and if they can't accept me for who I am, then I don't need them. If they want to hold grudges and so on, *screw them*.

And I have felt so much better, it felt great to move on and accept all of that and to tell my aunts off, and more. It took me years to do it but I did it. I have a past. I was a wreck for years, I made mistakes, I was troubled for years and more. I made mistakes, I lived, learned, moved on, I have changed, and more. It's other people's problem if they can't see that. Those are the people that I don't need in my life anymore and never did. They're the ones I leave in my rearview mirror and never look back.

CHAPTER
EIGHT

When Luke found all of that out, it did not go well. He was pissed that I found someone else and that I was pregnant. He still thought that eventually I was going to come back to him. He took our boys for a weekend in August and then didn't see them again until a weekend in October. On Thanksgiving Day, I told my boys they were going to see their dad the next day.

My youngest broke down; crying and panicking. I asked him what was wrong. He told me that his older half-brother touched him. My son's oldest half-brother has a record of touching and raping. I told Luke right from the beginning to never leave the boys alone with him and to always supervise them. But of course, Luke didn't listen to me, and now look what happened.

Then my oldest son told me that he was raped by their half-brother. They said they told their dad the same day it happened, but he didn't believe them. Luke called my boys liars. I started crying and immediately reported it. I then filed for full custody of the boys because enough was enough. I gave Luke enough chances to be a father to my boys, but he kept failing and hurting them. I was not going to let it happen any longer.

All he kept doing was making sure my boys kept getting hurt. Now he is going to pay and lose our boys for good. After all this was reported, shit hit the fan. Luke made threats to me, his first ex-wife made threats, and my boys and I were stalked. My boys were terrified, and more. I

15

called the cops, but they did nothing since it was a family dispute. I went to court and got full custody.

I told CPS once the case was set and I had the go signal that I would be leaving the state with my boys, my newborn baby girl, and my fiancée. So, once it was over, we left. We left the state to protect my boys and myself, to have a better life, and to start fresh.

It was hard and sad that it came to us leaving the state, but it was for the best. We didn't deserve to keep living like that.

CHAPTER
NINE

It was not easy after leaving the state, but we all knew that we could not look back. So, for a little while, we lived with my fiancée's brother until we found a place. We were in Alabama at this time.

Three months after leaving the state, I got a phone call about the sexual abuse case. My boys' older half-brother got one year in prison and ten years' probation, and my boys have a protection order on him until they're eighteen years old. Yes, evidence was found and proven that he did that to my boys.

I had my own feelings—I blamed myself. I'm beyond pissed that Luke put them in that danger and more. My boys are in counseling to help them heal. It took a while, but our new start started to come together. My boys were happier, and they were my boys again. Luke has not seen the boys since this has happened. It has now been two-and-a-half years.

My boys hate their father, and I don't blame them. They are domestic violence survivors and sexual abuse survivors like me. I am not happy or proud that they have been through all that. I never wanted that to happen to them. As a mother, you never want your kids to get hurt. As a mother, you want to always protect them.

I can't change the past. All I can do is change their future by giving them a better life now, be there for them, and more. That's what I intend to do because I love them so much. I want the best for them. I do not want what they went through to stop them and so I will teach them that they can succeed in life, have a happy life, and so much more—no matter what—because I've done it and they can, too.

I am going to teach them to be strong. It destroys me every day knowing that my boys have been physically and sexually abused. I never ever wanted any of that to happen to them. All I ever wanted was to give them a better life, but I failed them.

I will never fail them like that again. I can't change what they have been through, I can't take their pain away, but I will be here for them and I will get them through this. Their life will be so much better and that's a promise that I will follow through on.

CHAPTER
TEN

Living in Alabama is a challenge, but I love the weather because it has absolutely no snow. However, it's more expensive.

When we finally got into our own house, believe me, we struggled. Keeping a job in Alabama is even harder. You do one thing wrong, you're fired. It could be something small, and it would not matter. I went through many jobs and so did my fiancée.

Trying to keep a job in Alabama is not easy. We lived in our house for six months and we were behind on rent because when we did have jobs, we barely made enough to live on. The pay in Alabama is so low. We eventually got evicted. Then we moved into a hotel room, barely able to keep it paid. So, this is when things got bad between my fiancé and me.

He was always gone and never around. I could never reach him on his cell. He was around other people all the time. I got fed up with it, and I left him. My kids and I went and stayed with some people. My now-husband went through hell and more when we split up. He was homeless and living in a van for a while. He lost the van shortly after. He then slept anywhere he could.

He would sleep at laundromats, on benches, at a friend's house, even on empty houses, or trailers. He did anything he could to make it. He said it was the worst thing he had gone through. He said he would never go through something like that again. He said losing me was beyond worse than anything he had ever experienced. He said finding out he had cancer stopped him in his tracks.

He said it felt like he got hit by a train. Shortly after leaving my fiancé, I got a job at Chick-fil-A. That was when he found out he had stage one brain cancer. It broke my heart, and my world stopped. I could not believe it—the one man who was my true love was sick.

I loved working at Chick-fil-A. I looked for my own place but struggled finding one because the landlords in Alabama were very picky with who they rent their place to. The people I was staying with became controlling, nosy, and more. I was getting fed up with them.

During this time, my fiancé and I were talking again, trying to decide if we wanted to save our relationship and get back together.

When things went down were I was staying, I moved out. My fiancé and I, along with our kids, moved into another hotel. I had to quit my job at Chick-fil-A because I had no vehicle and I had no other way to get to work.

CHAPTER
ELEVEN

We bounced from hotel to hotel for a little over a month until we could not afford them anymore. We got a vehicle a month later. It was a convertible Volkswagen and I loved that car. Later, I sold it and bought an RV camper for my family, so we now had a place to live in. It wasn't the greatest, but it was ours and we had a place.

After three weeks of nonstop trouble with it, we junked it.

We went to another hotel for a few weeks. It got to the point where we could not afford it at all. We were then homeless and staying in shelters. My fiancée and I felt like failures at this point because we had hit rock bottom. Our kids didn't deserve this and it hurt us knowing our kids were going through this.

The positive side to all this was that we became more thankful. It was a huge eye opener and we learned a lot. We got a good taste of it in a different way and had a different point of view.

We were at this shelter for a few days. We had asked the supervisor to spread the word that we needed to get to Michigan for my fiancé's treatments, and she did. They blessed us with bus tickets to move to Michigan so that my fiancé could get his cancer treatment.

We were happy that we cried because we were blessed. It was a relief because, at that moment, we knew he was going to make it and that he had a chance to survive.

My fiancé's friend was supposed to let us stay with him until we got back on our feet, but he cancelled an hour before we got to the Michigan drop-off. Angry and panicked, we didn't know what to do. Again, we felt like failures. We thought we were going to lose our kids, thinking that this was the end.

CHAPTER
TWELVE

We reached the dropped off in Michigan and were stranded at the bus stop, not knowing what to do or where to go. Regretting coming to Michigan, my fiancé and I were ready to go back south. After hours at the bus stop, and nonstop calls, my fiancée was able to find a place for us to go. Campus of Hope for Families.

It was another shelter, but they help families stay together and help them get on their feet and stay on their feet. They help families apply for help through the county and more. Relieved, we started to cry because we knew right then and there that we were going to make it. We would be together and not lose our kids. So, it was the new start for us that we had been wanting because Alabama did not work out very well. It had been a living hell.

Michigan was going to be the new and better leaf we had been hoping for since we left New York. We arrived at the Campus of Hope at 7 p.m. that night, dog tired. Most of the staff were nice but some were very rude—the same as the residents. But we had a place, we were together and that's all that mattered. One week after we arrived in Michigan, we met some pastors.

Shortly afterwards, we got married. The nice pastors paid for our wedding. It was the best day of our lives. We did a justice-of-the-peace type of wedding. We were beyond happy, and it was what we wanted. Even though there were some good and bad things about the Campus of Hope, I would recommend them to anyone because they treat you like family.

They really seriously care about you. They don't lie; they don't tell you what you want to hear. They also helped us, and they opened our eyes. They changed how we handled things. We were beyond broke and beyond rock bottom. They helped us—by building us and our life back up. They gave us the positiveness that we needed.

CHAPTER
THIRTEEN

We had been at the Campus of Hope for three months now. The rules were really strict and more people were coming in. We were accomplishing a lot, and my husband was working. We were happy and doing a lot better until we learned that Luke and his crew had found us again.

They even tried to get inside but didn't succeed, *thank God*. Shortly after this, we left the shelter and went to another hotel knowing we could keep the room paid, with my husband working now.

We were at the hotel for three weeks when we got great news that we were accepted for rental assistance and they would pay for the security deposit as well. An answered prayer from up above. When we arrived in Michigan, we started going to church and started praying more, and this has helped us so much. It made us both better people. We started to heal, let things go, and more.

Going to church changed us. We gained back our faith, which we had lost. We started looking for a place to live. At this time, thanks to a church and women empowering women, we were able to have a small car. We were so happy. After a month of looking, we finally found a place and were beyond excited. We were getting on our feet, my hubby was working, and we were happy. We're having a baby boy—due on April 2021. Life was finally going great. Everything was coming together.

We didn't know what to do the first time we moved into our new home because it had been so long since we had a place. Our kids were beyond happy, and it felt great seeing their faces light up. After a year of hell and struggle in Alabama, we were finally able to accomplish what we wanted in Michigan.

Even though Alabama was hell and more, we were blessed that we got through it. I hope we never hit rock bottom again. Ever since we experienced being homeless, we have tipped our hats to them and gave more donations for them—because being homeless opened our eyes and taught us a lot.

Since we arrived in Michigan, my hubby became healthier. His cancer was more under control. It gave me comfort knowing that he was going to be around for a long time. He was strong enough to beat it. He is now gaining his weight back and is himself again.

When he got diagnosed with cancer, it brought flashbacks of my mother. It was hard, but I stayed by his side. My family stopped me from being there for my mother. I was not going to have that happen again.

Because of my family, I lost all that time with my mother. Because of them, my mother thought I didn't want to be there for her, when that was not the case at all. I blame them for that. Especially my one aunt that had me babysitting her kids constantly. She also ran her mouth about me, telling lies about me, and causing more issues. She would not know what to do with herself if she wasn't causing trouble for others. Ruining people's lives gives her a thrill. I blame my family, but I do not blame my sister.

CHAPTER
FOURTEEN

When we left state, my now-husband and I went through hard times like the ones I mentioned earlier in my story. I had left him a few times, but we got back together because we wanted to fight to save us and our relationship. We had struggled for a long time. We always found a way to work things out. Every relationship struggle, the ones that make it are stronger ones.

We always forgave each other and did not give up on one another. We can survive anything. A lot of our problems was our past, because of what I went through with Luke and what he went through with his ex. We found a way to help each other and now we're married. Our wedding day was the best day of our lives.

We didn't have much of a wedding, but it was all I ever wanted because, with him, it's not about a big wedding, or fancy dress, or any of that. It was about us and our love, about us becoming husband and wife. I have never felt this way before about a man. It is like when you try to describe something but can't find the words. When he looks at me, when we kiss, it's like fire. We also have another baby on the way, and we are so happy and madly, deeply in love. Yes, we still have our troubles but we stick it out together, we have learned a lot, and more.

I would be so lost without him. He has showed me what a real man is, what real love is, and what a relationship is like. He has taught me so much, he has also showed me what real life is really like. I never thought

I could trust a man or any of that again. I am so blessed that I could and I couldn't be happier.

I was beyond broken and more. He fixed me, put me back together. I love him so much. I have put him through a lot, I have hurt him, and so on. I can't say sorry more than I already have, and he forgives me each time; he stays because he loves me just as much.

I have had days to where I believe he deserves better than me. But I am the one he wants now and forever. I am the person he will always love no matter what. He has put me through a lot as well. He has hurt me, he has put me through hell, and so on. But, as he loves me, I love him just as much. He is all I want, and I choose to stay with him.

When I say we have hurt each other, I do not mean physically but verbally, with harsh words, with mistakes each of us has made that hurt the other one. I know I can always count on him to be there just like he can count on me to be there. That is what true love is and always will be.

I have not had this comfort since my mom died. He has not had this comfort since his grandmother died. And we both comfort each other now. I truly believe we were meant to be together. I am so blessed that he came back into my life. I truly believe my mom and his grandmother brought us together and kept us together no matter what we say to each other, or what we put each other through. It's 100% true love.

Here's a song that I wrote for my new husband, that I have plans on publishing someday. This song is about my new husband, it is also a song in loving memory to my mother. It's about how I felt after she died. How I didn't have a home after she died. How I used to run and more. But then he came back into my life and how he gave all that back to me.

Title – "Home"

I used to have a place called home
home is only a four-letter word, but to me it means so
much more
home holds my happiness, my sadness, where I go when
I'm hurt, and she was always there
then my mom died after her long, brave battle with
cancer
but now she's gone
all I do now is run
after that I had no place I could call home I was so lost
because I had no place to call home
until the day you came back into my life after all of my
running,
I finally found you, ever since you and your love have
been so amazing
you showed me that I was able to have a place called
home again
you also have shown me that I didn't have to run no
more
that I have a home again
where I can have happiness again, a place for sadness
again,
a place where I can go to hurt again, and you will be
there like she used to be
now I know that you will be there just like she used to be
You took a broken girl who was lost and had no one to
run to
no place to call home and gave me a place to call home
again
after all of my running I'm finally coming home

CHAPTER
FIFTEEN

Like I said earlier in my story, after my mom died, my sister and I lost contact due to many reasons. She was going through a lot and so was I. Our family didn't help with matters. So, for years we had very little contact and it hurt so much. I thought about her every day and missed her so much until we finally reconnected again; I was so happy.

I told her we needed to stay a part of each other's lives no matter what, and to not let the family tear us apart, and not to lose touch, etc. We need to remain sisters, remain in contact, and more. And she agreed. We are all we have left and I have nothing bad to say about her. She has always been there for me even when she wasn't and the same with me for her.

She has turned out great like me. She's now a mother as well. She has a good man. She's a strong person like me, because we got our strength from our mother. I am so proud of her and I know she's proud of me even though she does not say it. I know our mother is proud of both of us. We both agreed to see one another as much as we can as well as to have our kids be close to each other.

I look forward to the memories we both will make together. Not a day goes by that we don't miss our mother and how much we want her back. But we have our memories with her; her pictures. We both do the best we can because we know that she's watching over us.

CHAPTER
SIXTEEN

Shortly after we left the state, Luke, my boys' half-brother, and their crew found us like I mentioned earlier in my story. They knew where we were because they followed us. My boys' half-brother followed us and knew where we are all the time. We called the cops and they were aware.

I knew they wouldn't stop until they got what they wanted, and that was to hurt me and my boys. However, I didn't want to keep moving to different states. Since we left New York, we had lived in three different states. That was not fair to me, or my boys, or our family. So, we got legal protection. My boys and I never go anywhere alone. I still make sure my boys are happy and I do what I can so they're not terrified.

This is the price my boys and I have to pay for marrying a bad man who does not give up and who has connections. I don't believe he will succeed in hurting us, but I cannot tell further. I am doing everything I need to be safe—being armed legally and more—because I will not let him win. The cops told us that eventually they will give up. They have looked for them but have not found them yet.

The cops told us if Luke and his son keep stalking us, then we need to keep calling the cops or consider moving to another state, but that's not fair to us because we are the victims. Because of all this, I had to work from home to always be with my boys. My husband works at a real job, but I got a lot of locks on the doors and windows, I got protection, and 911 on speed dial.

Living like this is not fun, and not easy. It's hard and it sucks. But I have to do what I have to do for my family. I will never give up. I am so blessed to have my husband by my side during all this.

It means so much to me that my boys and I have him. I don't know if the cops will ever catch Luke and his crew, but I cannot lose hope that they will. Even when he and I were going to court before I left the state, he was still saying that he loved me even though I knew he didn't. Because Luke didn't know what love was. Back then, I guess I didn't, either. I do know one thing—I know what love is not.

CHAPTER
SEVENTEEN

With everything I have gone through, I always turned to my writing. Growing up, I always wrote. When I was with my ex-husband, I wrote. Even until this day, I write. It just seems to help me. I write poems and songs about my life, my experiences, and more.

Yes, I was touched, raped, beaten. I have no family, I'm a domestic violence survivor, I have been homeless, and hit rock bottom a lot of times in my life. My life hasn't been easy, but it has taught me a lot. It has made me who I am, it has showed me that life is not always roses and sunshine. But I never turned to drugs or alcohol.

I got out of my situation, I got help, I had support, I was on meds for a little while, I talked to others, I prayed, and so on. I was always able to stay as a great person. I am a great mother with a great heart. I admit I used to be ashamed of my past, embarrassed, and so much more, but not anymore.

It's all a part of me; it has made me the great person I am today. I share my past, my experiences with others for so many reasons. I have accepted it all; it's a part of me and always will be. I am not ashamed of my past or experiences. I share my past and my experiences to help others and to let others know that they are not alone and never will be.

If they're in a bad situation, they should get out of it and get help. You are strong enough and, no matter what, don't let your past or experiences make you an evil person. You can still be a good person. You can still have a good and happy life. You can succeed. Look at me,

I am happy, I am a great person and a wonderful, amazing mother. I have succeeded, and I have an amazing husband now.

Just because you have gone through something horrible, you should not let it control your life and destroy you forever. After you leave your situation, see a counselor, talk to others, read books about it, pray, and be positive. You cannot change your past or your mistakes, but you can learn and move on. It will always be a part of you. Don't let who ever hurt you win.

Don't give them the power to own or control you. Instead, use your power to show them that you are strong. Let them see how they lose and you win. Again, I cannot change my past, I cannot change my experience, but I can change and control my future. I can keep my head up, smile, keep doing what I'm doing now and more. If I can do it, I know others can as well. I hope that my story inspires others, help others, give others courage and hope.

Always remember to never give up. I have not and I never will. Let your past and the ones who doubt you give you power to keep pushing forward. Keep pushing forward for yourself, too. By giving up, you're just giving them what they want; do not do that. You can and will be so much more. It took me years to do all this and to accomplish it all, but I did it. If I can, anyone can.

CHAPTER
EIGHTEEN

Here's what I have accomplished in my life that I want to share with you. I have my own blog site and I have a country song being published. My true life story is being published and is going to be out there helping others. I do plan to publish more. I now have an amazing second marriage to an amazing man. I have my kids and another baby due in April 2021.

When I look back at my past, all that I have been through, I smile and say, "Wow, I am one hell of a strong woman. Look at what I have gone through, been through. I did it."

When you read my story, do not feel sorry for me. No, none of that. When you read my story and finish reading it, use my story as an inspiration, let my true life story help you and encourage you—as I said in the beginning of my story and throughout my story.

Every day, there are more and more abuse cases. Some are lucky to survive, but some are not so fortunate. If I did not leave my ex-husband when I did, I would have been one of the not-so-fortunate ones. I thank God every day that I got out when I did. Because it was just a matter of time before my ex-husband succeeded on killing me.

After being in that situation myself, and finally being able to speak about it, I want to help others, inspire others, and hopefully save others. Abuse has got to stop and go away. I tend to keep doing what I am doing because it makes me feel good knowing that my experience and my story could save a life, help someone, and let others know they're not alone.

The healing after being abused will not be easy. No, you may never be the same. You will heal, but the abuse will always be a part of you. But you're alive and you can move forward. You can accomplish anything if you put your mind to it. There's more to life than abuse. You do not need to be abused to have a life, you can live a life without the abuse.

There is always going to be something that brings up flashbacks of your abuse and your past. Believe me, I go through that, too. But I just stayed strong, held my head up, and kept moving forward. It's not worth going over it anymore, and it's not worth giving up.

So, even with my flashbacks, the nightmares, my ex-husband stalking me, I am still strong enough to keep moving forward, to keep smiling, to stay as a good person, a great mother, and a loving wife to my husband. I keep accomplishing what I want in life. I will not let any of that stop me, no matter what.

CHAPTER
NINETEEN

I admit that when I turned eighteen, I had my life planned. I had dreams and I had goals. I never expected to meet Luke and go through all the abuse. I don't regret any of it. The only blessing out of it all are my boys. If I never met Luke, I wouldn't have my boys and I would be so lost without them.

What Luke put me through just taught me more about life and how cruel men can be, but not all men. After being abused, I gained a backbone. I learned to speak my mind and I also learned to stand up for myself. But being abused also lowers your self-esteem big time. I still struggle with that, but I am getting a little better with that. I keep working on that every day to try to build my self-esteem back because in a little way, I know that I am pretty.

I look at my boys and all I can do is smile. When I have my days of wanting to give up, I look at them and they give me all I need to remind myself that I can't give up. They—my husband and our kids—are the reason I can't give up. I have come way too far. Some days it does cross my mind to give up, I am not going to lie. But I never will.

Luke may have changed how I live today, but I am alive. I have my husband, my kids, my friends, and my sister. I also have everything that I am accomplishing and more. So, even though Luke and his crew follow us, that's not ever going to stop me from having a happy life.

So, just remember that you will have days of wanting to give up. You will be different after your situation, but do what I do and look at all that you have. Count all the reasons why you can't give up and try hard to stay positive. What also helped me was praying, writing, my blog site, music, and more.

Find out what makes you feel better, so when you feel like giving up, it can stop those negative thoughts quick.

CHAPTER
TWENTY

I don't expect to save or help everyone out there who are being abused. I don't expect to encourage all of them and so on. If I do happen to save some, help some, or encourage some, then at least I saved some. It's true that not everyone who are abused wants to be saved or helped. I was the same way. I used to tell people that abuse is all I deserve, but I was so wrong.

Luke brainwashed me so bad that I used to truly believe that his control and abuse were all there was to life. That was just his way to make sure he kept me where he wanted me to be. I was his punching bag, his property. I do not miss the abuse or the control because now that I have experienced life without it, I now know what real life is.

Yes, I admit I am still afraid that I will be hit again or thrown again. Loud voices of men still trigger a horrible flashback and put me in a panic. So, yes, there is still a lot that I have to work on.

When I was with Luke, I lost everything. I lost who I was. I lost a lot of friendships because of him. I had no one to blame but myself because I stayed in that situation and allowed him to do all that. I was terrified, frightened, afraid, and more.

When I was with Luke, I had an eating disorder and only weighed 105 pounds. He used to always say that women were meant to be skin and bones, that fat women will never be wanted. He always told me if I got fat, he would tie me to the back of the tractor and make me run to keep up for me to lose weight.

I have learned since then that no matter how much you weigh, you are beautiful. You will find someone who will love you the way you are and that you don't have to be skin-and-bones to keep a man. Every woman is beautiful, wanted, and more in their own way. That's what makes us all unique and stand out. We all need to always remember to never let any man bring us down and make us believe that we're less than what we are.